AWESOME ACTIVITIES

COOL CIRCUITS

Susan Martineau and Nick Bushell
Illustrations by Martin Ursell

WINDMILL
BOOKS
New York

Published in 2012 by Windmill Books, LLC
303 Park Avenue South, Suite #1280, New York, NY 10010-3657

Adaptations to North American Edition © 2012 Windmill Books, LLC
© 2012 b small publishing ltd

Library of Congress Cataloging-in-Publication Data

Martineau, Susan.
Cool circuits / by Susan Martineau and Nick Bushell. — 1st ed.
p. cm. — (Awesome activities)
Includes index.
ISBN 978-1-61533-366-0 (library binding) — ISBN 978-1-61533-404-9 (pbk.) — ISBN 978-1-61533-481-0 (6-pack)
1. Electricity—Juvenile literature. 2. Electric circuits—Juvenile literature. I. Bushell, Nick. II. Title.
QC527.2.M355 2012
537.078—dc22
2010052112

Manufactured in the United States of America

CPSIA Compliance Information: Batch #BS2011WM: For Further Information contact Windmill Books, New York, New York at 1-866-478-0556

Contents

Before You Begin

Most of these experiments give you pretty immediate and incredible results. Some of them take a little longer and need more patience, but they are worth it!

You will be using lots of household items like salt, water, plastic cups, paper clips, and so on. However, you will also need to buy a few inexpensive things from an electrical or hobby electronic store.

Read through the whole experiment before you begin. If it doesn't work first time, try again! Remember that the circuits have to be done exactly as they are described. You could keep notes or even draw up your results like a real scientist or inventor.

Remember never to play with electricity in the plugs and sockets in your house. That can be very dangerous.

> You will need a bit of grown-up help in one or two places. These have been marked with this special symbol. **!**

Simple Stuff

We are the ELECTRONS.

Electricity flows a bit like water. Water is controlled by putting it through pipes and storing it in tanks. Electricity is controlled by running it through wires and storing it in **batteries**.

When electricity flows, little bits of matter called **electrons** move through the wire. Electrons are very small. You cannot see them, but you can see the effect they have on things. In this simple circuit the little electrons are moving so fast and there are so many of them that they make the bit of wire in the lightbulb get hot and glow.

What you will need:
- 1 9-volt PP3 battery
- 1 red crocodile clip lead
- 1 black crocodile clip lead
- 1 4.5-volt lightbulb and bulb holder

1 Screw the lightbulb into the bulb holder.

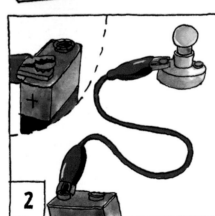

2 Clip one end of the red lead to the positive (+) side of the battery. Clip the other end to one side of the bulb holder.

3 Clip one end of the black lead to the negative (−) side of the battery.

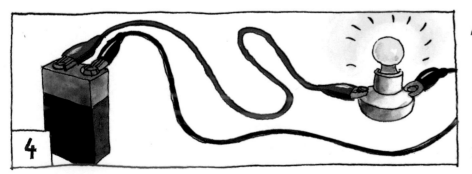

4 Clip the other end of the black lead to the free end of the bulb holder and see the bulb light up!

Croc Clips
It doesn't really matter what color the crocodile clip leads are. It just helps us to explain what you need to do!

Watch out!
They can pinch!

Batteries

Batteries have a positive (+) and a negative (-) side. These sides are called terminals.

BRIGHT SPARK

The first electric light bulb was invented in New Jersey by Thomas Edison in October 1879. As a boy he had been expelled from school because his teacher thought he was stupid! By the time he was ten years old, Edison had set up his own laboratory. In the years to come, he would also invent the world's first machine for recording sounds.

The Electrons

Electrons have a negative charge. Therefore, they flow from the negative (-) side of the battery to the positive (+) side through the circuit. Electrons are attracted to positively charged things. The amount of force that the electrons flow with is measured in volts. That is why we talk about the voltage of a battery.

I'm feeling very negative today.

Pencil Power

What happens if you add a pencil to a circuit? Imagine water flowing through a nice clear pipe. If you put a bit of sponge in the pipe the water would still be able to go through, but the sponge would slow it down. In a circuit a pencil will do a similar thing—it will slow the flow of electrons down. It's what is called a **resistor** in electrical circuits. Resistors make sure just the right amount of electrons are delivered to each part of a circuit inside electronic gadgets like TVs and computers. Without them, it would be like having a water tap that can only be either switched off completely or blasting out water with no way of slowing it down.

What you will need:
- 1 9-volt PP3 battery
- 1 red crocodile clip lead
- 1 black crocodile clip lead
- 1 green crocodile clip lead
- 1 No. 2 pencil, sharpened at both ends
- 1 4.5-volt lightbulb and bulb holder

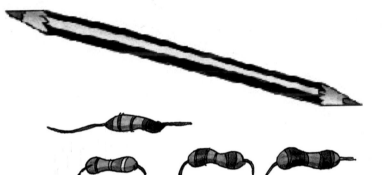

The Electrons

What are the electrons up to in this circuit? In a simple circuit with very low resistance, the electrons can whiz around quite easily. The pencil resistor here is making it more difficult for them. It's as if they have an obstacle in their path. It's like battling through a military obstacle course.

CONTROLLING THE FLOW

Resistors are all around us! All the electronic stuff in your house has resistors inside it. Some of these resistors are even made from carbon, the same substance that is inside the pencils we've just used!

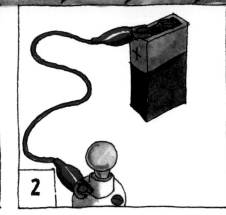

1
Screw the bulb into the bulb holder.

2
Clip one end of the red lead to the positive (+) side of the battery. Clip the other end to one side of the bulb holder.

3
Clip one end of the black lead to the negative (–) side of the battery. Clip the other end to one end of the pencil.

Clip to lead of the pencil.

4
Clip the green lead to the other end of the pencil and to the free side of the bulb holder.

The bulb will not glow as brightly as it did in the last experiment. You can test this by removing the pencil and reconnecting the circuit without it.

Resistors in Action

Now have some fun making different types of circuits using pencil resistors. You can try doing it with more than two pencils each time if you like.

Two Is More!

First we're going to make a parallel circuit. Connect the battery, bulb, leads, and pencils as seen below.

What you will need:
- 1 9-volt PP3 battery
- 7 crocodile clip leads
- 2 No. 2 pencils, sharpened at both ends
- 1 4.5-volt lightbulb and bulb holder

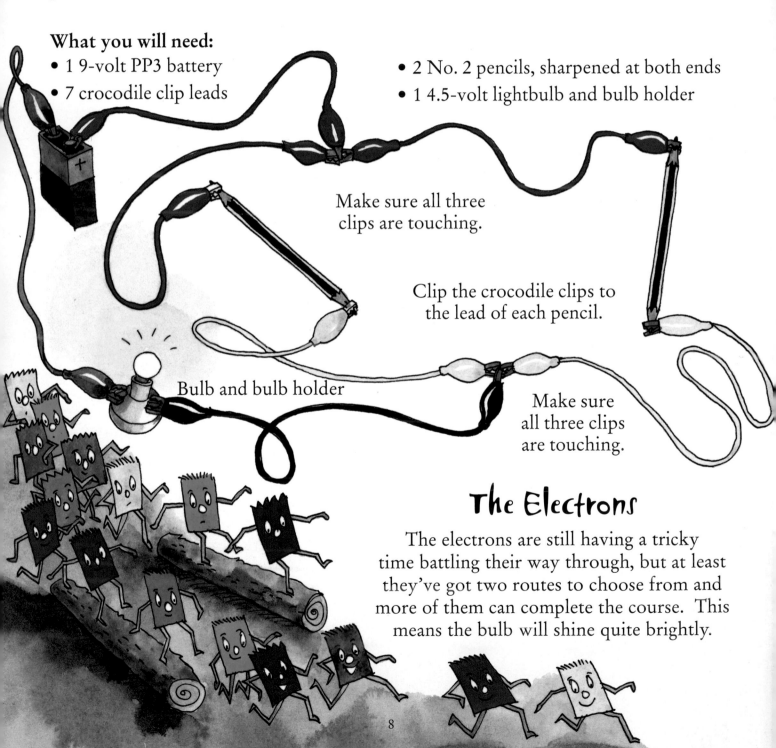

Make sure all three clips are touching.

Clip the crocodile clips to the lead of each pencil.

Bulb and bulb holder

Make sure all three clips are touching.

The Electrons

The electrons are still having a tricky time battling their way through, but at least they've got two routes to choose from and more of them can complete the course. This means the bulb will shine quite brightly.

Two Is Less!

Now try making a different sort of circuit with the pencils in line with each other. This is what is called a series circuit. Set up the circuit as seen below

What you will need:
- 1 9-volt PP3 battery
- 4 crocodile clip leads
- 2 No. 2 pencils, sharpened at both ends
- 1 4.5-volt lightbulb and bulb holder

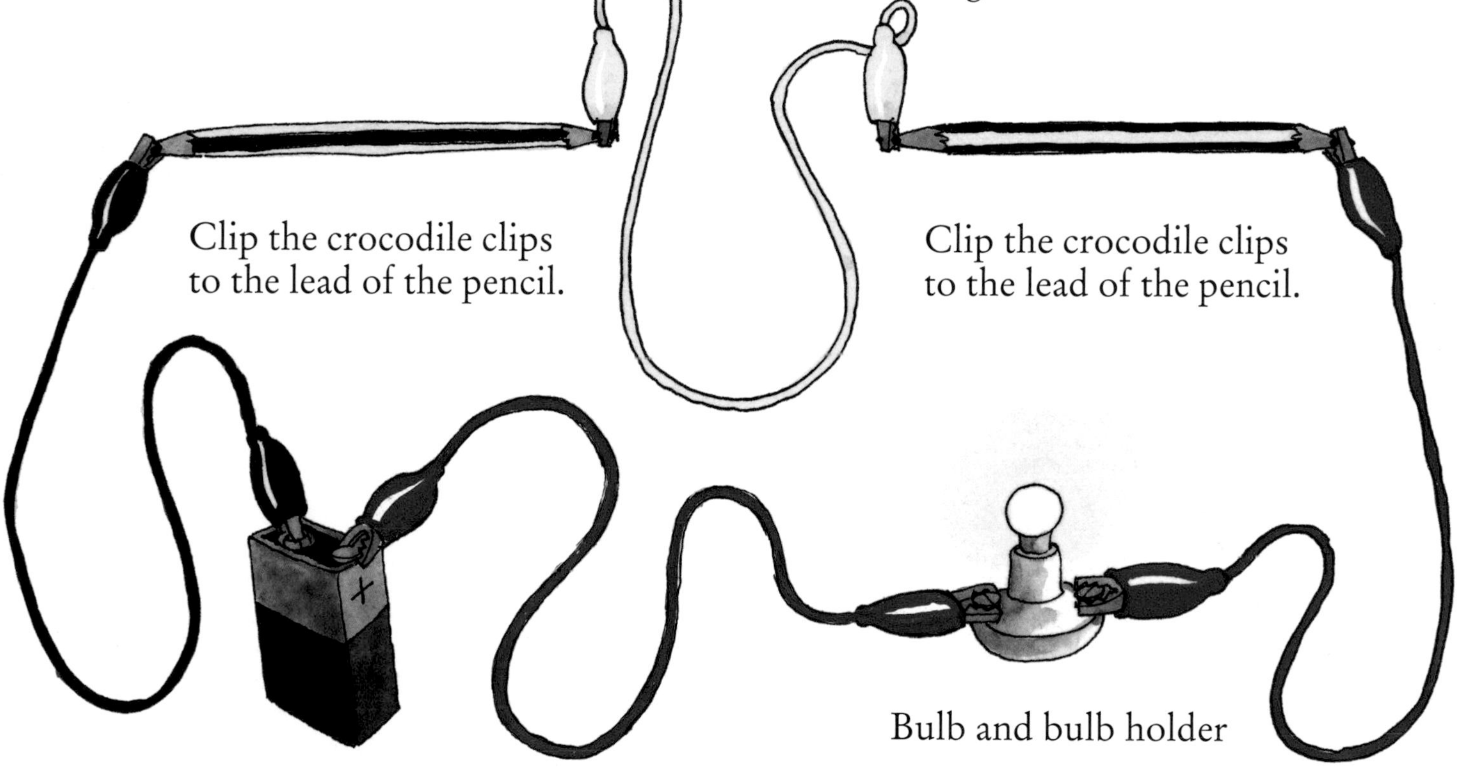

Clip the crocodile clips to the lead of the pencil.

Clip the crocodile clips to the lead of the pencil.

Bulb and bulb holder

The Electrons

This time the electrons are faced with a longer route. They have to fight their way through with only one possible path. The bulb will not shine as brightly because not so many of them can get through at a time.

OHM'S WORD IS LAW

Resistance is measured in ohms. They are named after a German scientist called Georg Simon Ohm. He did a lot of work on electricity but met resistance from people who didn't think his ideas were that important!

I just want to go Ohm!

Colorful Circuit

The lightbulb is a fantastic invention, but it is now being replaced in lots of equipment by a special electronic component called a Light Emitting Diode, or LED for short. LEDs are made by an incredibly tricky process that makes the lightbulb look as if it belongs in the Stone Age!

You can buy LEDs quite cheaply in electrical stores. They come in all sorts of colors. The great thing about LEDs is that they don't need much electricity to light them up. In fact, if you didn't have a bit of paper towel to act as a resistor in this circuit, the battery would be too powerful for the LED and it would get zapped!

LEDs have one leg that is shorter than the other!

positive (+) side

negative (-)side

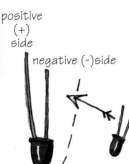

WARNING!
Do not touch a battery if your hands are wet! It might give you a little electric shock.

Salt

What you will need:
- 1 9-volt PP3 battery
- 1 red crocodile clip lead
- 1 black crocodile clip lead
- 1 green crocodile clip lead
- Small piece of paper towel
- 1 LED (any color)

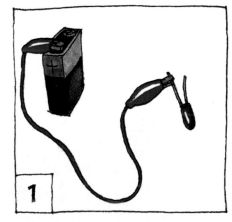

1

Clip one end of the red lead to the positive (+) side of the battery. Clip the other end to the long leg (+) of the LED.

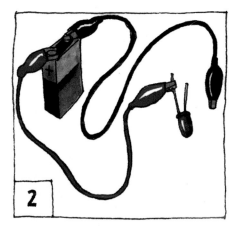

2

Clip one end of the black lead to the negative (-) side of the battery.

3

Fold the piece of paper towel into four layers.

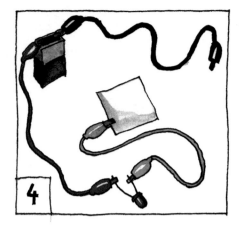

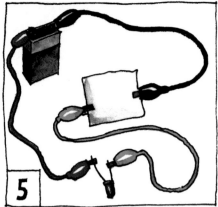

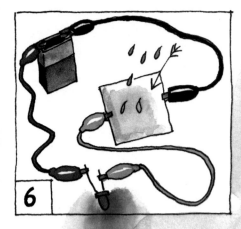

Clip one end of the green lead to one side of the paper towel. Clip the other end to the short leg (-) of the LED.

Clip the free end of the black lead to the other side of the paper towel.

Sprinkle a little bit of water on the paper towel until it is soaked through. Watch what happens to the LED.

Salty Circuit

Sprinkle some salt on the wet paper towel. See what happens to the brightness of the LED.

The Electrons

What do the electrons do inside LEDs? When an **electric current** is running through an LED, it's as if the electrons inside it are jumping off a diving board. Instead of making a splash of water, they each give off a splash of light. The voltage from the battery pushes them up to the top of the board and then wheee! They fall down and give off their splash of light. The dry paper towel on its own won't work, it has too much resistance. When you sprinkle some water on it, though, enough electrons can get through to light the LED. If you put salt on the towel as well, even more electrons can pass around the circuit because the salt reduces the resistance of the water. The LED glows even more brightly.

11

Briny Battery

You can make your own battery using salty water and coins! It will produce enough electricity to make an LED work. A cheap red LED will work best. This simple, homemade battery isn't quite powerful enough to make a lightbulb work. This is why LEDs are so handy. They don't use as much electricity.

What you will need:
- 6 crocodile clip leads
- 1 red LED

- 5 plastic cups
- 10 teaspoons of salt

- 5 pennies
- 5 squares of aluminum foil, 2 inches (5 cm) by 2 inches (5 cm)

1 Fill each plastic cup halfway with water. Sprinkle two teaspoons of salt into each cup.

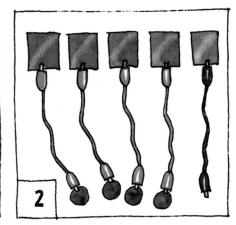

2 Clip a separate lead to each aluminum square. Clip the other ends of four of these to four of the coins.

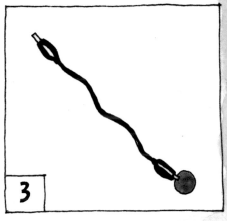

3 Clip the sixth lead to the last penny.

OOZING BATTERIES!

The chemicals inside batteries are not nice. They have names like cadmium, manganese dioxide, ammonium chloride and lithium thionyl chloride. They are definitely not good for you. Sometimes batteries will leak inside your electronic equipment. If you can see that something has oozed out of a battery, you must dispose of it carefully. Then wash your hands really well.

The chemicals in batteries can harm the environment when they are just thrown away in our trash. Try to find out if your town has a special place where batteries can be disposed of safely.

4 Line up the cups. Place the foil squares and coins inside them as shown.

Make sure none of the foil squares and coins touch inside the cups.

5 Place the coin that is on its own lead in one of the end cups.

6 Place the foil on its own lead in the other end cup.

foil

coin

7 Connect the free end of the lead attached to the coin to the long leg (+) of the LED.

8 Connect the free end of the lead attached to the foil to the short leg (-) of the LED.

Turn off the lights. You will be able to see the LED glow!

Try This!

To make your battery really strong, see if you can get the foil and coins as close as possible without touching each other.

The Electrons

Your briny battery is creating a chemical reaction which releases electrons. Each cup of salty water containing a coin and foil gives the electrons more energy. It's as if each cup is a rung on a ladder, and the LED is the diving board. When you have enough rungs, the electrons can reach the diving board and jump off, making their splashes of light as they do so.

13

Mighty Magnet

Did you know that where you've got **electricity**, you've got magnetism too? When electrons move around they make a **magnetic field**. You can use this to turn an iron rod, like a screwdriver, into a magnet. You need to coil some wire around the metal and connect it to a battery. The more wire you coil round, the stronger your electromagnet will be.

Your screwdriver may still pick up light objects, such as paper clips, even when the electric current is switched off. This is because it is possible to make the screwdriver permanently magnetic!

What you will need:
- 1 9-volt PP3 battery
- 2 crocodile clip leads
- 13 feet (4 m) of insulated wire
- 1 medium screwdriver with a plastic handle
- Scissors
- Tape
- Paper clip

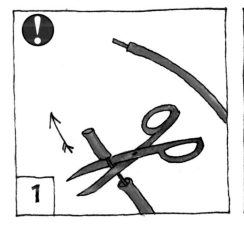

1 Use the scissors to strip a small bit of plastic from each end of the wire.

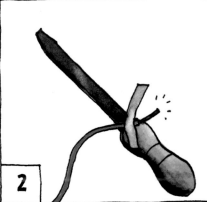

2 Tape one end of the wire to the handle of the screwdriver. Do not touch the stripped wire with the tape.

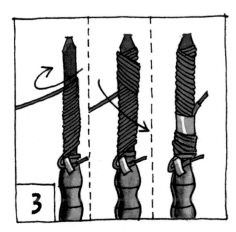

3 Wrap the wire as neatly as you can around the metal part of the screwdriver to make a coil. Go back over the first coil to make a second one. Tape the wire to hold it in place.

SCRAPYARD MAGNETS

Powerful electromagnets are used in many industries to lift and move really heavy metal objects. In junkyards, they can be attached to cranes to lift scrap metal, such as old cars.

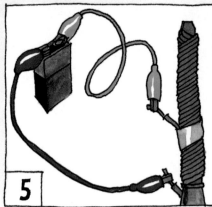

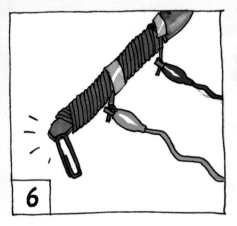

Clip one end of a lead to one end of the coil. Clip the other end of this lead to the positive (+) side of the battery.

Clip one end of the other lead to the free end of the coil. Clip the other end of this lead to the negative (-) side of the battery.

Try picking up the paper clip with the screwdriver. Remove a crocodile clip from the battery to switch the magnet off.

WARNING!
Make sure the battery does not get too warm! It's best to disconnect the battery after a short while.

The Electrons

When an electron moves, you get a little magnetic field. If all the electrons move together, as they do when moving through a coil of wire, you get a very strong magnetic field. In the coil, the electrons are all whizzing around, just like in a corkscrew on a roller coaster! If you keep the electric coil on for long enough, the electrons in the screwdriver also start to move in a synchronized way. It's as if they have been taught to line dance!

Cool Compass

You can make your own **compass** by magnetizing a needle. The sort of magnet you need for this is a bar magnet with an N and S marked on it to show you the north pole and the south pole of the magnet. When you compare your results with a real compass, you will be amazed!

What you will need:
- 1 needle
- 1 bar magnet
- Small piece of paper towel
- 1 plastic cup
- Compass (for checking purposes only!)

1

Fill the cup with water. Take the needle between your thumb and index finger.

2

Hold the magnet in your other hand with the north end touching the eye of the needle.

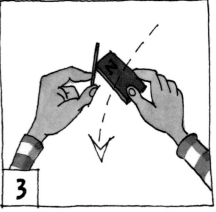

3

Stroke the north end of the magnet down the needle starting at the eye end. Do this several times from the eye to the point.

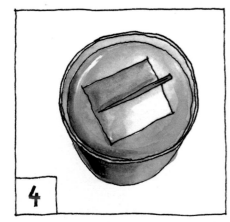

4

Float the piece of paper towel on the surface of the water. Gently place the needle on it.

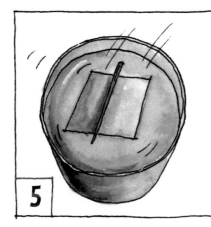

5

Watch the needle and paper towel turn on the water. The eye of the needle will point north!

Get your real compass. Check if the compass you made is working.

MEGA LAVA

Inside Earth, there is an enormous mass of swirling molten rocks and metals. These rocks and metals flow in a particular pattern. This movement creates an electric current. This amazing electric current also makes a magnetic field in a particular shape. Using incredibly powerful computers, scientists have been able to recreate the shape of this magnetic field. We call the top of this shape the magnetic North Pole and the bottom the magnetic South Pole. A compass tells you which way is North and which is South.

Magnets also have a north pole and a south pole. The south end of a magnet will be attracted to the north end of another magnet. Therefore, the south end of our magnetized needle is attracted to Earth's magnetic North Pole!

MYTHICAL MAGNETS

There is a story about an Ancient Greek shepherd boy called Magnes. He was out tending his flocks when the iron tip of his crook and the iron nails in his sandals got stuck to the ground! He had found stones containing a naturally magnetic mineral which we now call magnetite. However, magnetite was likely really named after an area called Magnesia, which is now in Turkey. Loads of these rocks can be found there.

17

Crazy Currents

We can make a nifty gadget to show there is an electric current flowing through a wire. If we put a compass inside a coil of wire attached to a battery, the compass will move. This is because of the magnetic field created by the electric current in the wire.

What you will need:

- 1 9-volt PP3 battery
- 2 crocodile clip leads
- 13 feet (4 m) of insulated wire
- Scissors
- 1 small compass
- Plastic top from an aerosol can
- Tape
- Poster putty or plasticine

1 Use the scissors to strip a little bit of plastic from each end of the wire.

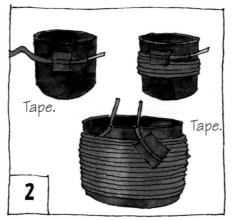

Tape.

Tape.

2 Tape one end of the wire to the can top. Wind the wire around the can top. Make a second coil on top of the first.

Position the north and south arrows along the edge.

3 Put a blob of poster putty or plasticine on the back of the compass. Push it down on the edge of the can top.

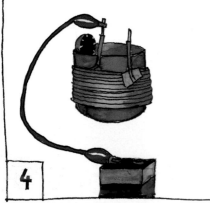

4 Clip one end of a lead to one end of the wire coil. Clip the other end of this lead to the positive (+) side of the battery.

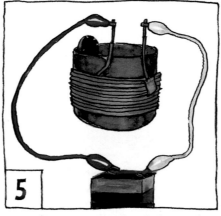

5 Clip one end of the other lead to the free end of the coil. Clip the other end to the negative (-) side of the battery.

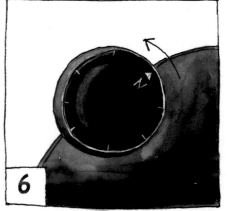

6 The compass needle will swing in one direction. This shows you that there is a current passing through the wire.

Try This!

Now swap the clips so that you change the terminals they are clipped to. Watch the compass needle swing in the opposite direction.

FATHER OF THE AMP

You have likely seen the word amp on electrical bits and pieces. Amps are named after a scientist called André-Marie Ampère (1775–1836), who studied circuits. Electrical currents are measured in amps in the same way that the length of something can be measured in inches (cm). An ammeter is the name of the gadget which measures them. Electronic ammeters are used in lots of portable equipment, like laptops and cameras, to work out how much longer the battery will last.

The Electrons

What are they up to now? The electrons are whizzing around the coil of wire as if they were on a roller coaster. When you switch the clips on the terminals of the batteries, they all change direction and zoom round the roller coaster backwards! This then makes the compass spin the other direction.

Break-dancing Magnet

In Crazy Currents, we used a compass to show that there was an electric current. Electricity can also be used to make a noise. We can do a wacky thing with a magnet on some thread to show this movement. Use the can top with the wire around it from the previous experiment. Remove the compass first, though.

To make a sound that our ears can hear, the movement has to be very fast and it has to move a lot of air. In a loudspeaker, there is a moving coil connected to a cone-shaped piece of paper that helps the loudspeaker move the right amount of air so that our ears can hear a noise—or music!

What you will need:
- 1 9-volt PP3 battery
- 2 crocodile clip leads
- Can top with wire coiled around it from page 18
- 1 small round magnet
- Scissors
- Poster putty
- Cotton thread

1 Put the can top on its side.

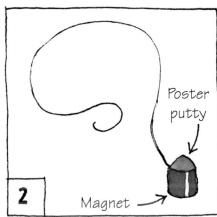

2 Stick the magnet to the end of a length of thread using a blob of poster putty.

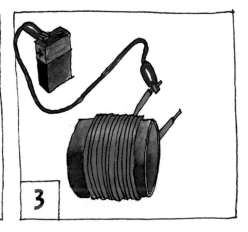

3 Clip one end of a lead to the positive (+) side of the battery. Clip the other end to one end of the wire coil.

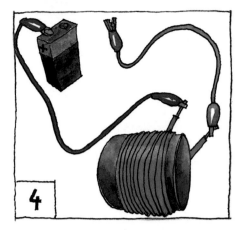

4 Clip one end of the other lead to the free end of the wire coil.

5 Dangle the magnet on the thread in front of the open end of the can top.

6 Touch the negative (-) side of the battery with the unattached crocodile clip.

Watch that magnet dance!

WAVES OF SOUND

A microphone works in the opposite way from a loudspeaker. It turns small movements from the sound waves of someone speaking or singing into an electric current. This current is so small that it is difficult to do an experiment to show how it works without doing more tricky electronics.

Radio Magic

In your circuits you have controlled electricity by using wires to get it to go where you want it to. This is not the only way electricity moves, though. Electricity can also jump through the air if it has enough energy.

You might have seen a very small spark when you were connecting the crocodile clips to the battery in the experiments. (Try making a circuit in the dark and see if you can see a small spark when you connect the battery.) This is electricity jumping through the air, just like lightning does during a storm.

Electrons flowing through a wire create a magnetic field. That is only half the story, though. Electricity and magnetism are so closely related that if the electrons are made to change directions and go up and down a piece of wire, they can actually make an electric field on top of the magnetic field. This is called an electromagnetic field. Radio waves are one of the things this produces.

A radio receives electromagnetic waves sent out, or transmitted, by a radio station. The radio makes them into electrical and then sound signals that you can hear. Here's how to make a very simple radio transmitter by turning an electrical current on and off.

What you will need:
- Radio
- The circuit from Simple Stuff on page 4

1 Switch your radio to AM. Tune it so that you cannot hear any music or talking.

2 Put the radio near your circuit. Turn the circuit on and off. (Tap one of the sides of the battery with the crocodile clip.)

3 You will hear clicks in time with the flashing of the bulb even though the circuit is not connected to the radio by wires!

The Electrons

What about the electrons here? When the circuit is switched on, the small spark is like the electrons doing a massive cannonball dive into a swimming pool. The big wave they make travels through the air and is picked up by the radio. The electrons in the antenna of the radio start going up and down with the wave from the big splash. It's just like you would if you were floating at the other end of the pool when the wave from the cannonball hit you.

SPEED OF LIGHT

Light is also an electromagnetic wave. Radio waves and light waves all travel at the same speed. This is called the speed of light and is about 670 million miles per hour (300 million m/s). That means it takes a light wave one third of a millionth of a second to go 328 feet (100 m). Sound waves take one third of a second to move 328 feet (100 m)! It takes the Sun's light about 8 minutes to reach Earth.

23

Read More

Bartholomew, Alan. *Electric Gadgets and Gizmos: Battery-Powered Buildable Gadgets that Go!* Kids Can Do It. Tonawanda, New York: Kids Can Press, 1998.

Flaherty, Michael. *Electricity and Batteries.* Science Factory. New York: PowerKidsPress, 2008.

Somervill, Barbara. *Electrical Circuits and Currents.* Sci-Hi: Physical Science. Chicago: Heinemann-Raintree Publishers, 2008.

Glossary

batteries (BA-tuh-reez) Things in which energy is stored.

compass (KUM-pus) A tool made up of a freely turning magnetic needle that tells which direction is north.

electric current (ih-LEK-trik KUR-ent) A flow of electricity.

electrons (ih-LEK-trons) The parts of atoms that have a negative charge.

magnetic field (mag-NEH-tik FEELD) A force made by currents that flow through metals and other matter.

resistor (rih-ZIS-tor) A thing that blocks or slows down a force.

Index

Web Sites

For Web resources related to the subject of this book, go to: www.windmillbooks.com/weblinks and select this book's title.